GREYWOOLF

RANDY GREYWOOLF

GREYWOOLF

autobiography

TATE PUBLISHING
AND ENTERPRISES, LLC

Greywoolf
Copyright © 2013 by Randy Greywoolf. All rights reserved.

No part of this publication may be reproduced, stored in a retrieval system or transmitted in any way by any means, electronic, mechanical, photocopy, recording or otherwise without the prior permission of the author except as provided by USA copyright law.

This book is designed to provide accurate and authoritative information with regard to the subject matter covered. This information is given with the understanding that neither the author nor Tate Publishing, LLC is engaged in rendering legal, professional advice. Since the details of your situation are fact dependent, you should additionally seek the services of a competent professional.

The opinions expressed by the author are not necessarily those of Tate Publishing, LLC.

Published by Tate Publishing & Enterprises, LLC
127 E. Trade Center Terrace | Mustang, Oklahoma 73064 USA
1.888.361.9473 | www.tatepublishing.com

Tate Publishing is committed to excellence in the publishing industry. The company reflects the philosophy established by the founders, based on Psalm 68:11,
"The Lord gave the word and great was the company of those who published it."

Book design copyright © 2013 by Tate Publishing, LLC. All rights reserved.
Cover design by Jan Sunday Quilaquil
Interior design by Honeylette Pino

Published in the United States of America

ISBN: 978-1-62854-837-2
1. Biography & Autobiography / Personal Memoirs
2. Biography & Autobiography / Religious
13.10.21

In loving memory
of Mom and Ma Maw

TABLE OF CONTENTS

Introduction 9
Early Childhood 11
The Call and Rejection 13
The Descent 15
My Teen Years 17
The Setup 19
The Vision 21
The Baptism 25
The Visitation 27
The Decision 31
My New Family 35
Reuniting With My Family 41
Year of Fasts 45
My Grandfather 49
Smokescreens 51
You Shall Be Called "Greywoolf" 53

Guard Your Heart 57
Pease Park (Please let it be dry) 59
Visited by Indians 63
The Pallet 65
Fifty-Day Fast, God Chooses the Music 67
From the Author 73
Child of Light 75

INTRODUCTION

The story you are about to read is true. The events have actually happened over the course of my life. I have written them in this book in hopes of encouraging all those that are children of light and those who have yet to become children of light. "He is waiting."

> 1st John 1:5: "This then is the message which we have heard of him and declare unto you, that God is light and in him is no darkness at all.

> Ephesians 5:8: "For ye were sometimes darkness but now are ye light in the Lord: walk as children of light".

> Psalms 42:1: "As the hart panteth after the water brooks, so panteth my soul after thee, O God.

EARLY CHILDHOOD

It was a cold and rainy day. Mom had called Ma Maw because she wanted some of her homemade stew. She was not feeling well, and I was told by Ma Maw to take the stew to her. I was about ten years old, and we were living upstairs in a duplex apartment. I remember how the thunder rolled and the lighting flashed outside. I was in no hurry to make the delivery. Ma Maw had called and said, "Come get the stew and take it over to your mom's." I picked up the stew and opened the door at the top of the stairs. I shut the door behind me. As I stood at the top of the stairs by myself, I asked God to please not let the thunder or lightning get any more terrifying than they already were, at least not until I reached mom's apartment. And with that, I proceeded to scurry down the flight of stairs.

As I reached the bottom, I opened the door and ran as fast as I could without spilling any of the stew and cornbread. As I ran, I couldn't help but notice how quiet it was. I was about three blocks to mom's apartment. She also lived upstairs.

When I had reached the top of the stairs and opened the door, I realized there hadn't been any thunder or lightning anymore. As I went in, I turned around, faced outside, and thanked God for not letting the lightning or thunder roll in. And with that came one of the loudest claps of thunder I've ever heard. That was God's way of telling me "You're welcome." This was the first time I had asked God for something.

THE CALL AND REJECTION

It was a Sunday morning and everyone was at church, except for my grandfather. It was an exciting service. A lot of people were down at the altar, crying and praying. My mom was down on her knees, crying to the Lord. I went down and cried too. I was about eleven at this time. After the service, I walked home by myself. It was a nice warm day, and as I was walking, I felt the presence of the Lord. At that time, I felt like he wanted me to surrender my life over to him, to take up my cross and follow him.

The thing was, as far as a kid's life goes, mine was pretty good. I lived with my grandparents by myself, had all the toys an eleven-year-old could want and had all the love that my grandparents could give me. My grandmother was the best cook I ever knew, so I always ate well. I had plenty of friends and won almost all the games I ever played in such as football, soccer, baseball, among others. Things always went my way. It wasn't that I did not believe in the Lord, it was just that I did not want to change anything in my life at the time. I knew I wouldn't be able to do things his way and my way at the same time. So I knew I had to make a choice, his will or my will. I chose my will. He always gives us a choice.

THE DESCENT

It was not long after that things started to change. New kids had moved to my school. They were bigger and seemed older than most of my classmates. I started to see things differently. My childhood seemed to have passed without anyone letting me know about it. I started getting into trouble at school—talking too much, food fights in the lunchroom, and just getting into more trouble in and out of school. My will was starting to shine, not of obedience but of disobedience. After the school year had ended, we moved out of the city to a farm in the country. I would start the eighth grade there. My childhood days were the best days of my life, and they were over.

MY TEEN YEARS

We moved to a 360-acre farm. There were plenty of chores to do. We had a three-acre yard which we mowed by hand, and I had the job of trimming all the fence line. There were no weed eaters back then. We also had about thirty fruit trees that I trimmed around every time we mowed while my grandfather cut the field with a bush hog mower. The place needed a lot of work, but my grandparents were looking out more for my best interests. They figured I wasn't as likely to get into trouble, and they were right.

Our closest neighbor was about a mile away. My grandparents took care of the farm for free rent and a meager salary. My grandmother took a job about twenty-five miles away as a waitress at a small country café. I eventually joined her at the café, and worked about three nights a week. I waited tables, washed dishes by hand, and mopped the floors. I also took money at the register and cleaned the grill, which smelled like rotten eggs, with grill bricks. Every morning, I rode the bus to school and was usually the last one on and the first one off. I didn't play sports anymore though. We lived too far from school for my grandfather to come and get me after practice every day. But I still loved sports and played every chance I got with friends from school.

We had also two dogs; one of them was a beagle and the other a St. Bernard. I would play hide and seek with the beagle and lay a trail for him to follow. The trail would go around the house, in the barn, back to the tool shed around the car, and then back in the house. I stood at the door and watched him chase the trail. He would always find me.

After a while, my grandfather got the place in shape for the owner to buy some cattle. He bought about sixty cows and two bulls. We cut and baled hay in the summer. Those were some hot summers. I remember one summer my grandparents and I were all working together, hauling hay. My grandmother and I threw the hay on the trailer while my grandfather did the stacking. He put the tractor in low gear and pointed it between the rows of hay. My grandmother was something special though. She never once complained about all the hard work that was required in the farm. She was an inspiration, but I still had not surrendered my will for the Lord's will.

THE SETUP

How excited I was to have my mom ask me to spend the summer with her, my sister, stepbrothers, and stepfather. My mother was now living in Louisiana. I had just turned sixteen and the school year was over. My stepdad had gotten me a job on a shrimp boat with someone he knew. I was going to earn some money so I could get me a car to drive. It was my first night out on the boat. We were going to an oil rig to pick up a crew and bring them to shore. My stepdad dropped me off at the boat earlier that evening then we left and headed for the oil rig.

It was just me and the captain. I didn't know it then, but it was about sixty miles offshore. I didn't know how far out we were in the ocean before I started getting sick. Not only was I sick, but the worst thing you could have ever imagined had also happened. I was molested that night; I was in a place that had no way of escape, nowhere to run and nowhere to hide. I never expected that anything this terrible could ever happen to me. I was just supposed to be working so I could buy my car when I returned home. The things that took place that night were done to put me into bondage and destroy my soul. They destroyed my innocence and left me feeling ashamed. My stepdad knew, he was the one that set this up. But little did he know that God would not let this destroy me. God would heal my soul and in time break that yoke off of me.

When summer was over and I was back at home with my grandparents, I started smoking weed. The guilt and shame were never far away. It seemed as though I could never get rid of them no matter how much I tried. By the time my senior year arrived, we had moved out of the farm. We were now living closer to the café where my grandmother and I were working. We lived in a small two-bedroom-wood-framed house. My senior year went on, with me spiraling down fast with weed, alcohol, and pornography.

I wanted to play football. I now had my car, and the football team needed a little help. There was only one problem—I was always high, even during classes at school. It seemed like I never came down. I remember one time at the pep rally before a game started, the cheerleaders called out player's numbers and said something about them. My number was twenty-two, and they said I was loaded. And they were right. Even at that moment during the pep rally, I was loaded. I got to the point where I woke up one morning, looked in the mirror, and didn't recognize myself. For the first time, the thought of suicide crossed my mind.

THE VISION

It was in the middle of the night when I found myself outside. I was looking up at the sky, and there were these bright lights shining down. I could see a myriad of colors in the lights—red, blue, green, among others. I looked at them directly as I was standing at the corner of our house out in the front yard. The next thing I knew, I was on the rooftop, looking across the roof. I realized I was directly above the middle of the house, still looking at these lights. Then suddenly, I felt as if the lights were going into my stomach. They filled me up and started to overflow. It was like perfect peace, perfect love. I felt completely whole. The only thought that came to my mind was, *Wow, this is what I've always wanted.* It was his love, perfect and pure, and I knew it. And then I saw myself across from me. My face was glowing, my teeth were straight (at that time in my teenage years, my teeth were crooked). It was the real me, Christ in me, the "Hope of Glory." A huge smile was plastered on my face, and I did not remember anything after that.

The next morning at school, I felt so happy. It was not until my fifth period class that I remembered what had happened. I did not tell anyone about it since I was really not sure what had happened. It wasn't long after that I suddenly felt a hunger for God's word. I started reading the Bible. I read in the book of Proverbs a lot. Shortly after I started reading the Bible, I asked the Lord to come into my life, wash my sins away, and save me. I did this in my bedroom, with me down on my knees, when no one was around. I was seventeen at the time, and ready to surrender my will for his will. Now, I could not wait for the change to come. I wanted to be like the person I saw in my vision.

However, change didn't come so fast. Before school was out in my senior year, I got arrested and put in jail twice for public intoxication. My eyes were being opened concerning the laws of the land. I wasn't doing any harm to anyone or anything, but nevertheless I was breaking the law. During the end of my school year, I started talking to some of my friends about the Bible. I remembered during lunch we would drive off campus and go get us a hotdog and a drink. We would talk about the mark of the beast and the end of the world stuff. However, I was not delivered from my drinking and smoking yet.

By the end of my senior year, I was ready for my school year to be over. My grandparents moved to east Texas shortly after I graduated. I moved to Dallas to stay with my mom and work. I got on at a truck place where I cleaned out and vacuumed tractor trailers. I worked there for a little while, but it wasn't long after until I was back living with my grandparents in east Texas. They were taking care of someone else's property again, and had their own trailer to stay in. I had my own room and I acquired a job working as an orderly in a nursing home in this small east Texas town. I fed, shaved, and bathed those that I was responsible for in the nursing home. Some of them were physically challenged while others were mentally ill. It was difficult to see all the dilemmas that they were going through.

THE BAPTISM

It was a cold January day, and by then I had been reading my Bible a lot. I had read that Jesus was baptized by John the Baptist, and I knew that's also what he wanted me to do. I was going to a little country church down the road from where we lived. I went in that morning and asked if I could be baptized. The preacher said yes, but the baptistery was not working at the time, so he asked if it would be all right with me if we could go down to the pond instead. And I told him that it was. So after the service, I went home and got a towel and some extra clothes to change into. I didn't know it at the time, but there were several other people that wanted to get baptized as well. I don't really remember too much about my surroundings, but I do remember that it was cold. The preacher took me out to the pond until I was about waist-deep then put me under the water. When I came up, something had changed; I could actually feel my old self being buried and the new one rising up out of the water. I felt so clean and whole, and it was truly wonderful.

THE VISITATION

Shortly after I was baptized, I had a visit from the Lord. I had just woken up and was lying there in bed just thinking. All of a sudden, I felt like someone was in the room with me. It was a small bedroom and I didn't see anyone come in. I kept looking around the room, but I still didn't see anyone. Then I heard a voice. "Truth, whatsoever things are true. Truth, whatsoever things are true," it said. Then the room felt empty, and it was just me lying in the bed, looking to see where the voice was.

I thought about what had just happened. I got up and went into the kitchen where my grandparents were drinking coffee. I told them what had just happened, and it left them with a puzzled look on their face. They did not understand it either. I thought I knew what it meant at first. I thought I was supposed to be in a band and we were to call it "Truth" and then just write songs that were true. But that was not what it meant. As I was reading my Bible one day, I came across the book of Philippians:

> And finally brethren what so ever things are true, what so ever things are lovely, what so ever things are of good report, if there be any virtue or praise think on these things).
>
> Philippians 4:8 (KJV)

I knew then. It was the spirit of truth that I had heard in my room, and it was about to take me on an adventure that would change my life forever.

While still working as an orderly in the nursing home, I also kept reading my Bible. One day, I read a passage that said:

> "Therefore I say unto you, Take no thought for your life, what ye shall eat, or what ye shall drink; nor yet for your body, what ye shall put on. Is not the life more than meat, and the body than raiment? Behold the fowls of the air: for they sow not, neither do they reap, nor gather into barns; yet your heavenly Father feedeth them. Are ye not much better than they?" (Matthew 6:25-26)

> "But seek ye first the Kingdom of God, and his righteousness; and all these things shall be added unto you." (Matthew 6:33)

I remember playing Frisbee in the woods where we lived. It was so peaceful and quiet. I had time to think about all the things I was learning. I went out, made up my own course, and kept score. I made up different shots—around this tree, between those trees, over these trees, down to the left or to the right of another tree. It was a fun game, and I thought to myself, *This could be a real game someday.* But at the time, it was just mine.

THE DECISION

"But seek ye first the kingdom of God, and his righteousness; and all these things shall be added unto you" (Matthew 6:33). This scripture tugged at my heart. But how do you seek the kingdom of God?

"Man cannot live by bread alone, but by every word which proceedeth out of the mouth of God." (Matthew 4:4)

No man can serve two masters; for either he will hate the one, and love the other; or else he will hold to the one, and despise the other. Ye cannot serve God and mammon" (Matthew 6:24). I didn't fully understand what this meant, but I knew at this point and time in my life I had to make a decision to either follow Jesus or follow the world. To follow the world was a normal way of doing things—having a job and getting a steady paycheck. Following Jesus was not having a job and doing whatever he told me to do. I chose to follow Jesus.

Soon after I made my decision, my grandparents were faced with a tough choice. Their landlord told them I couldn't stay with them anymore, even though I hadn't done anything wrong. But my grandparents couldn't move at such a short notice, so they suggested I stay with the Gentles for a while. They were a Christian family, so my grandparents thought maybe they could help me understand what I needed to do. They drove me to the Gentles house. It was about two hours away. When I got there, I still had no idea what I was going to do other than to just follow the Lord. The Gentles were very nice people, but they were not real sure what they were supposed to do with me either.

One of their children, who was in their forties, worked at a big plant in town. It was a soup company, and they figured they could get me in there, at least until I understood what the Lord had in store for me to do. They loaded me up one morning and took me to the soup plant where I would fill out an application and go to work. But when they were about to pull up to the guard shack, I told them that this was not for me. They didn't know what to do, so they just took me back to their house instead. Now, they had to figure out what to do with me.

The Gentles had been attending a small church in the town, and on Sundays and Wednesdays we would all attend. Apparently, I became a topic of conversation in the church, and one afternoon, I was asked to have lunch with a family that also went there. They had three boys and one girl that were still living at home. After lunch, we sat around talking, and then they decided to ask me if I would like to come live with them. I didn't really see that coming, but I was not surprised by it either. After all, I had figured the Gentles we're not sure what to do with me, and I guessed they thought this family might know. I didn't know this at the time, but this family had often taken kids into their home until something else came up for them. So I said yes, I would like to move in with them.

"I love them that love me; and those that seek me early shall find me" (Proverbs 8:17). Indeed, I had found where the Lord was leading me to, for he also said, "Thou wilt keep him in perfect peace, whose mind is stayed on thee: because he trusteth in thee." (Isaiah 26:3, KJV). I was at peace and truly felt his peace with this family. I was in my early twenties at this time. They themselves had just moved to this town. They had a business where they came from, but they chose to leave everything behind. The Lord had told them to follow him as well.

MY NEW FAMILY

"For whosoever shall do the will of God, the same is my brother, and my sister and & mother". (Mark 3: 35). He was teaching me this by firsthand experience. I lived with this church family for about three and a half years. We went to church a lot. They didn't try to tell me how I should act or what I should be doing with my life. They just let me grow in the Lord. I didn't realize I was growing in him, but I was. I remember once when they told me, it took me about two weeks before they saw me smile. I guessed I was just a little worried about what would happen next. After all, this was all new to me. I had never done anything like this before.

We lived in a house that had three bedrooms, and their boys and I stayed in one bedroom, with bunk beds. Apart from me, they also had two other boys living with them, and one of them was going to college. His parents lived in South America while the other boy's parents lived in the same small town as we did. While their kids went to school, I took time helping around the house. The family I was living with was also helping a disabled student get to college. And it was fortunate that they had a minivan because the student was in a wheelchair, and every time, I would help pick her up and set her in the van. We moved a couple of times while we were in this town. For a time, we had lived on Main Street. Every Friday and Saturday night, the street would all be backed up with cars from one end of the town to the other. It was mostly high school kids and college kids looking to have some fun. At that time in my life, I did not have a car nor did I care about getting one. The last place we lived in was on the outskirts of town. It was a small house, and I mostly slept on the couch. We didn't have much heat in the place. I remember waking up one morning and finding the glass of water left on the table frozen over night. I remember the Lord teaching me to be content no matter what circumstances I may be in. Whether there was plenty or lack, I was to be thankful.

I was still reading and studying the Bible a lot, and as I was, I witnessed a few things during this time. For instance, a traveling preacher came to our church and had a week-long revival. One night, our family cooked spaghetti for them and the other members of the church. We did not know how it happened, but we ended up with enough spaghetti that lasted for three whole days. I knew we did not have that much on hand to cook and knew too that we did not cook that much. This reminds me of the story where Jesus feeds the multitude of people from only five loaves of bread and two fishes. "And they that had eaten were about five thousand men, beside women and children" (Matthew 14:21).

Another time I and the two boys were on our way home from church. It was already night and we were just walking. We were all together side by side, with me in the middle, when suddenly one of the boys stopped. "Look," he said. We turned around and saw our shadows on this huge building. What caught our attention though was that my shadow was much larger than theirs. It was not because I was bigger or taller, because I wasn't. The building that our shadows were on was one of the biggest church buildings in town, and we thought there simply was no reasonable explanation for all the oddity with the shadows.

But we had some fun times as well. I remember once, we had a picnic in the park somewhere and finished up by eating a cold watermelon. I don't remember who started it, but bits of watermelon started flying all over the place. Everyone was throwing and eating, and it was hilarious. Toward the end of my stay, I remember waking up one morning and reading the Bible. The Lord spoke to me and said fast forty two days. I thought to myself, "Forty-two days?" I had never done fasting before, even for one day or two days, much less for forty two days. But I did like the Lord said. I drank only apple juice and water, no food. And then I remember a scripture where the Pharisees asked Jesus about why his disciples didn't fast. He said that as long as he was with them, there was no reason to fast, but the day would come when he would be taken and then his disciples would then fast.

I did not take the fasting lightly, I felt honored that he had told me to do it. I started the fast in the month of November, and it ended on New Year's Day, so I finished out the old year not eating. The day I ended the fast was also the same day that I ate again, so I actually started the New Year with a meal. It went well, I really didn't get hungry. After the first few days, I really didn't have much of an appetite. I felt like I was becoming a true disciple, one that would do what he was told to do. The fast was done during the holiday months, Thanksgiving and Christmas. I remember drinking warm apple juice during those cold winter months.

We spent Christmas in Arkansas. It was a snowy white Christmas. During the fast one night, I had a dream. I saw Jesus and he was clothed in a white robe and with sandals on. He was standing on a porch that had white pillars. He had a beard and his hair was long and brown. I couldn't believe it. I actually saw Jesus, my Lord and King. Even though he did not say anything, it didn't matter. Seeing him was enough. By the time my fast ended, I had lost about thirty pounds and looked rather skinny. I didn't know it at the time, but when it was finally over, so was my time with this family.

The family I had been staying with was moving to Oklahoma. On the night before the fast would be over, I had a dream. It was a sobering one. It was about my real family—my mother, brothers, sister, and grandparents. They were all standing in what appeared to be a flame of fire. I knew then he was about to send me back to my real family to be a witness for him. I decided to head back to Irving, Texas to stay with my mom.

Before I left to go, as I was standing outside our house, I saw three angels standing on the roof. They were not very big or well-defined. They were merely glowing figures, and I could almost see through them. They just stood there, not moving or talking. I thought it was simply remarkable; I had never seen an angel, or angels for that matter, before. When my fast was over, my spiritual family had taken me to stay with my grandparents. I figured I was not going to Irving just yet.

I was at my grandparent's apartment when I actually finished the fast. The morning the fast was over, my grandmother fixed me a small bowl of oatmeal, some toast, and a small glass of milk. I stayed there for a while until I got my strength back and went back to my spiritual family's house to get some transportation. They had not moved just yet. I didn't know then that the Lord had a surprise for me that would help me get around. Our neighbors down the road had a four-door, faded blue Datsun. They came to me and said that the Lord had told them to give it to me. I gladly accepted their gift. Now, I had a way to get around. I don't remember a big send-off, but I knew that my time there was over, and so was my spiritual family's. And somehow, I guessed they were sent there for me, as I was for them.

REUNITING WITH MY FAMILY

I was now staying with my mom and two brothers, who were in middle school and high school. I remember taking my younger brother to school in my car, and he would be so embarrassed by my car that I would have to drop him off about a block away from school so no one would see him in that car. The car wasn't much to look at, but it was truly a gift from God, whether or not anyone recognized it. And then I got a job cleaning carpets, together with a friend that I had known when I was in the small town of Paris, Texas, and had made enough to buy me another car. My little putter I had been using conked out on me, but it still had been a blessing and had gotten me back home where I was needed. It was not easy for me to be back home; I went from an environment of belief to one of unbelief.

I found a church to go to, and my mom even started going with me. We heard some good preachers at that church. From Irving we moved to Grand Prairie. My mom was working in a café in Oak Cliff. She had worked there for many years. My brothers changed schools, and I changed jobs. I worked at the five-and-dime store and also went to Bible College for a few semesters. My brothers and I also started playing tennis. We would play in tournaments together. This was a lot of fun for us, and our mom would come and watch us play. I remember one tournament where we were all lined up in a row in courts one, two, and three playing a match at the same time while mom was watching us. Those were some of the best times I remember with my brothers. My sister would also come watch us play. I really didn't feel like I was making much of a difference in their life at the time. I wasn't preaching to them or anything like that; I was just trying to live out my faith the best I could in front of them. I was not perfect by any means, but I was sincere in my walk with God.

Mom moved out of the apartment where my brothers and I were staying. We did not last too long by ourselves. My brothers went their way, and I was losing my way. One night, I drank and smoked a lot. And then I got very sick, and it took me four days to recover. When I finally gained my health and strength back, I got up and went to a park down the street. When I reached the park, I sat down on the ground in front of a little pond. The water was calm and there were even a few ducks there. As I sat there, I could hear the scripture in my heart and mind. "The Lord is my shepherd; I shall not want. He maketh me to lie down in green pastures: he leadeth me beside the still waters. He restoreth my soul.

He leadeth me in the paths of righteousness for his name's sake." (Psalm 23:1–3, KJV)

As I sat there, the spirit of the Lord was truly restoring my soul. I could feel his peace and presence. It was a calm that came over me, and I had not felt that peace in a while. I went back to work for a few days after that. One morning, when I was getting ready for work, the Lord again spoke to me. "Yesterday was your last day at work," He said. I was surprised and now wondering what I was going to do.

YEAR OF FASTS

---☀---

I was about to move out from the apartment, but I did not know where I was going to go. Mom was still working at the café in Oak Cliff. Mom had a customer who had a house out there and said that I could stay with him for a while. His name was Harry and he was in his eighties. My brothers went out and got them an apartment together not too far from where we had been living in Grand Prairie. Harry had a big house that he also rented out. Mom and I eventually moved into it and started paying him rent. My brothers followed us shortly and moved in. I was not working at this time. My Mom really didn't want me to. I stayed at the apartment and played a lot of tennis. During this time, the owner of the café where mom worked sold it to someone else. The new owner liked mom and wanted her to take on more responsibility. Mom was doing the buying, payroll, and managing of the café. I told her the Lord was getting her ready for her own café. She would laugh but would also believe it.

Now in the mid to late eighties, the Lord put me on a series of fasts. I say the Lord put me on the fast because it was his idea, not mine. I remember one time I went on a fast on my idea, not his, and I barely made it through one day without eating. I could not do it on my own, so after that I never went on a fast without him telling me. This particular year he had me on more fasts than I had been on in my whole life. I was not sure why he put me on them, but knowing that it was his idea and not mine was enough. The first fast he put me on went on for three and a half days with no water. I had never been on a fast without liquid of some sort, so this was a first. I was not sure if I could go three and a half days without drinking something, but I did.

The second fast he told me to do went on for seven days, and still with no water. Well, that one got my attention. Seven days without water and you may die. It was July and very hot, and I was also playing in a tennis tournament. The tournament ended on a Sunday, and I was to begin my fast on Monday. There was not much time to recoup or recover from the tournament. I remember this particular tournament because it was so hot the players were cramping, and one player even got dehydrated so bad the tournament director called an ambulance for him. The tournament was over, and I was now going home to get ready to start my fast. I was not sure how my body was going to react without water for that long, or that I could even go without water for that long. But I just trusted in the Lord that I would be okay, and I was. I made it through the fast. Water never tasted so good when I finally got to drink some. I am not saying I understood the reason for the fast, but I knew he ordained it and that was enough for me.

It was a few months later when he told me to go on another fast. I guess the first two were in preparation for this one. For this particular fast lasted for ten days. No food, no water. When the Lord said that, I could hardly believe it. Ten days without water would be impossible, but with God, I knew all things are possible, and if I was to survive this it would definitely be by his power. I did survive it though. And I know I could never have done it without his help. It was October and it wasn't as hot as it was in July. I didn't have anything I was praying for specifically, I was just being obedient to his word. I don't remember much about the fast, other than how good it had felt to take a cool shower after because during the fast your body temperature rises due to the lack of water. Also, time seems to come to a screeching halt. The hours seem like days because your body is screaming for water. When it was finally time to come off the fast, I remember taking communion. A little grape juice and a little piece of cracker were the first things I tasted. After that, I had breakfast and went to sleep.

MY GRANDFATHER

My grandparents were still living in the country, but my grandpa became ill and eventually passed away. My grandpa had lived a hard life. He was on his own at a very young age. He used to ride the boxcars to go from town to town. He was stationed in Germany while serving in the army during World War II. He married my grandmother while he was in the Army. My grandmother was much younger than my grandpa and her mother did not like that at all. One day, her mother even took an ax to his car to detour him from coming around. It did not work, and they ended up getting married anyway, and stayed married all their lives.

My grandmother also had some kind of condition, and the doctors told her that if she would have a baby it would either kill or heal her. My grandmother ended up having only one child, a girl, and her name's Francis Loraine Dobson—my mom. My grandpa wanted to have a boy too, but they never had any more children. I think that was why my mom was okay with me staying with my grandparents because she figured I was the son they never had. My grandfather loved baseball, and I remember when the Rangers moved from Washington and became the Texas Rangers. My grandfather took me and my friend next door to go watch them play. He also took my mom's boss's daughters to some of the games. There were so few fans back then that almost every time we went to watch a game; we would end up getting a baseball.

SMOKESCREENS

I had been invited to hear a man speak at some sort of meeting. His name was Alberto Rivera. He was an ex Jesuit priest. The meeting started at seven o'clock that night, and I was standing in the kitchen, washing dishes. No one was there, I was all alone. All of a sudden, there was a cloud in front of me. It was a small cloud of smoke, about three-by-six-feet, and had no smell. As I gazed upon it, I noticed heads of snakes popping in and then out of the clouds so that I couldn't see them. The vision didn't last long, but it sure was strange. And I did not know what it meant at the time.

I got ready to go to the meeting at six o'clock in the evening, and my friends came by to pick me up. I did not tell them about the vision that I had seen. The meeting began, and the speaker was a short man, who also had quite a story to tell. He was telling us how his religion ran. It was a religious machine. I was very depressed when I had left the meeting because of all the things he had told us. However, I also knew that they were all true. One of the reasons I knew this was because he was actually selling a book that was written by Jack T Chick. The book was called *Smokescreens,* and when I saw it, I understood why the Lord had showed me the vision; The Lord was showing me that what this man was saying was the truth.

YOU SHALL BE CALLED "GREYWOOLF"

My grandmother did not drive, so I went to the country in East Texas to stay with her for a while. I was in my late twenties then, and my main focus was to make sure my grandmother lived as normal and happy as she could. She was not sick or ill, she just could not drive or go anywhere by herself. I felt it was my responsibility to take care of her. After all, she and my grandfather had raised me, and this was the least I could do for her.

It was not always easy though. I had many sad days where I thought the world was passing me by. My sister was getting married and having children, and I didn't even have a girlfriend. The Lord had put me in a position where I was separated from the rest of the world. Mom, meanwhile, eventually got her café, still in Irving Texas. She was so proud; after twenty years of hard work as a waitress, she finally got her own café. The food was good, so it was no wonder that later on she began having a loyal customer base.

One morning, my grandmother and I decided to pay my mom a visit to her café. My grandmother was supposed to go to a doctor's appointment the next day, but since the doctor was close to where my mom lived, we decided to just spend the night with mom and then go to the doctor in the morning. That night, I went to see a movie, which was called *Dances with Wolves*. This was a rare occasion for me. When the movie was done, I went straight home and slept on the couch. It was in the middle of the night when something woke me up. As I opened my eyes, I saw three silhouettes standing in front of me. They looked like they were Indian, and they said, "You shall be called Greywoolf." I wasn't afraid or anything, I just rolled back over and went to sleep.

The next morning, my grandmother and I were at the doctor's office. As the receptionist was calling out names, she called out for a David Wolf. As soon as I heard that, I suddenly remembered what had happened last night. I didn't give it any more thought, until that one evening a month later when I was standing on the front porch of the apartment where my grandmother and I were staying in the country. I looked up in the sky, and it was clear and blue, except for this one cloud, which was right in front of me. It was a perfect picture of a wolf head, just as if someone had drawn it. It was looking straight at me. At this point, I decided to ask my grandmother what was going on with all of the Indian stuff. My grandmother told me that my great grandmother was Cherokee. She also told me that my great grandparents were from Tennessee and that they went to live in McKinney, Texas. And this was where my grandmother was born.

That's when I considered to actually changing my name. After all, it was biblical. The Lord had changed Abram's name to Abraham, Jacob to Israel, Saul to Paul. So now, I understood.

GUARD YOUR HEART

After my grandfather passed away, I stayed with my grandmother. We lived in government housing in a small east Texas town. My grandmother had a neighbor next door whom she was good friends with. Her name was Janie and she had a daughter named Santos. The apartment on the other side of Janie had been empty, until one day when a single mother and her two sons moved in. At this time, I had no girlfriend or even any prospects. I was alone and living with my grandmother. Well, needless to say, we became friends. We talked all the time, and it was this way for a few years.

Then one day, someone asked her out on a date, and she accepted. When she told me about it, I couldn't believe it. I was heartbroken because it didn't seem to matter to her. I was hurt and confused and I didn't understand how she could go out with someone when we were so close. Well, I figured it was mostly one-sided. It was me liking her more than her liking me. I figured it out after I had a dream one night. The dream began with me walking in this big room, where all the walls were filled with trophies in the form of different animals mounted on the walls. I kept walking when all of a sudden I saw something I couldn't believe. It was me mounted on the wall just like the other animals! I had become her trophy and there was nothing I could do about it.

I had been led away by my own lusts and desires, and this was the price I had to pay. The only lesson I came away with it was to never let this happen again. The pain lasted for years, but it gradually went away as time went by. "Keep thy heart with all dillgence; for out of it are the issues of life" (Proverbs 4:23). What a painful lesson that was.

PEASE PARK
PLEASE LET IT BE DRY

I was at a disc golf tournament in Austin, Texas one summer. My grandmother had passed away earlier that year. I was still living in East Texas working different odd and end jobs. I drove down and stayed with some of my disc golf friends since they were also playing in the tournament. I had never played this course before, but it was one of Austin's most played courses. It was a typical tournament. I had to be at the park around seven or seven thirty, loosen up, stretch, and then throw some of the holes to get familiar with the course. Everything was going pretty well after the first day. I was close to the lead, and after the third round I had the outright lead by a couple of shots.

We were nearing the end of the last round when I did something I had never done in a tournament before. We had only a few holes left when I suddenly stepped on the tee box and threw as hard as I could. The hole was about 450 to 500 feet away. The wind was blowing pretty hard, and there was a creek that ran through the park and by this hole. When I let go, I saw that the disc was heading for the creek. My heart sank as I watched the disc disappear into the ravine. It was a steep drop-off from the fairway. I had no way of knowing whether it was out of bounds in the water or safe on dry ground. It was then that I did something that I never do in a tournament.

I asked the Lord to please let it be dry. I have never asked him to let me win in a tournament. For me, it was enough that I play my best and just let the chips fall where they may. But never the less, on the way to my disc I did ask him to please let it be dry. It would almost certainly be a two-stroke swing if it were wet because I could not see the basket from the ravine and I had a thirty-foot drop-off to throw out from. As I got closer to the creek bed, my heart was racing, and as I made my way down toward it, my worst fear was realized. My disc was in the middle of the creek, not even close to being dry. I picked up my disc, dried it off, got my footing, and launched the disc in the general direction of the basket. It was about 200 to 250 feet away when all of a sudden I heard the guys on my card hollering. I couldn't understand them, but they were sure making some noise. As I climbed up out of the ravine, I saw what they were hollering about. My disc had found its way into the basket. They couldn't believe it and neither could I, but there it was, just sitting there in the basket, pretty as a picture.

Even though the disc was out of bounds, it did not matter. I got a three on the hole and not a four or a five. The Lord didn't do what I had asked him to do, he did much more. His ways are not our ways and his thoughts are not our thoughts. They are higher than ours.

I went on to win the tournament and I never told the story to anyone until now. God was listening; he always hears us, but sometimes he doesn't answer us the way we expect him to.

VISITED BY INDIANS

After my grandmother passed away, I left east Texas and moved to Irving, Texas. I took a job as a driver for a juice company in Dallas. I had several friends that worked there. One night, before I went to work the next morning, I had another dream. In the dream were two Indians, and they were wearing headgears and jewelry, along with their native apparel. They didn't say anything, but there was a mountain behind them and a trail on the side of the mountain that led to the top. I was thinking about walking up the side when I suddenly had a thought of needing to take my shoes off because the mountain was holy. After that, I woke up.

The next morning, I went to work. It was a typical day; I was picking up and delivering the products. I was in the warehouse when I saw two men being escorted by the owner. He was helping them get some snow cone syrup, and he introduced me to them. The men were from Oklahoma, and they were Christian Indians. When I found out about that, I couldn't believe it. These were the men in my dream last night! The men apparently were father and son. They were not dressed up in the Indian apparel I had seen them in last night, but I knew for sure it was them. I got to speak to the father briefly. He and his son apparently had a ministry and were here in Dallas to get snow cone syrup for their summer camp. Our owner, who was also a Christian, gave them what they needed with no charge.

I helped them load up, and in no time, they were on their way. Before they left though, the father gave me one of his cards. He told me to call him up some time. A month or so went by and I still could not stop thinking about the dream and the men in the dream. So one day, I decided to call him and asked if we could have lunch. He agreed. I drove to Oklahoma and met with him at a little café. We talked for about an hour or so, and when we were finished he told me I should write a book. I didn't say whether or not I would, but I just said I would think about it. But that wasn't the last time that I saw him. When the owner of the company where I had been working passed away, I called him to let him know. His son brought him to the funeral, and we spoke briefly. And I have not seen him since.

THE PALLET

The Lord answers our prayers, and sometimes, even before we ask. I know this because it happened in my life before.

One day while at work, I was supposed to pick up some material for production. I was driving the company's bobtail truck, and I picked up goods from a place I had never been. Before I left, I remember someone telling me to take a pallet with me for the pickup. That was no problem since we had plenty of pallets in the warehouse I could take. I arrived at the company where I was to pick up the goods around lunchtime. Some companies closed down for lunch. This one did, and I did not know it at the time.

When I went inside to speak with someone, I noticed on their window the company's written policy, which stated that no product shall leave their company unless the driver brings a pallet for exchange. At this point, I remembered I forgot to bring a pallet. How could I forget, it wasn't that hard to remember. But I did, I flat forgot. I got in my truck, wondering what I was going to do. It was too far to go back to our warehouse, so I left to go get me some lunch instead, and all the while hoping that when I got back, they would not require me to have a pallet.

I was looking for a place to eat when I spotted something on the side of the road. I drove right past it when I realized it was a pallet, a perfectly good pallet. No boards were missing; there was absolutely nothing wrong with it. I immediately pulled into a parking lot. I got out of my truck, walked over to where the pallet was, picked it up and proceeded to load it onto my truck. There really was not an explanation of why the pallet was there, but I knew why it was there. It was for me. I thanked the Lord immediately for I knew he put it there. I never even got to ask him for help yet, but he knew my thoughts before I asked. God is so good.

FIFTY - DAY FAST, GOD CHOOSES THE MUSIC

I had been working at my company in Irving, Texas now for almost ten years. My friends helped me get a job there after my grandmother had passed away. One of my friends had left the company and went to work somewhere else. We talked about his new job and how he liked it, and he told me I should try to get hired on too. I considered it for a while, and eventually I decided to give it a try. The pay was more than I had ever made, and the job had really good benefits. It was time to move on, and I knew it. I got the job and started orientation in a few weeks.

It was around January, and by this time I had a girlfriend. Her name was Debbie, and she worked at a dental facility in Dallas. The Lord had put us together, and we were following the Lord together. But we were about to go on a journey we had not seen coming.

After I finished orientation, I started my first day on my new job. It was good, I had a trainer who rode with me and who also happened to be a Christian. After the first day of driving, an ice storm hit the Dallas area, forcing some businesses to halt and close down—ours included. When it was time to go back to work, the Lord spoke to me. He wanted me to go on a fifty-day fast. This would be the longest fast that he had ever told me to do. I could drink apple juice and water, but no food. I knew that fifty days of fasting would deplete me of all my strength. There would be no way I could do the fast and go to work during those fifty days. What was I going to do? I had a mortgage and bills that I was responsible for. I had little money in the bank, and that was all I had.

Following Jesus is a daily choice, not a monthly or a yearly choice. You follow him one day at a time. (Joshua 24:14-15) "Now therefore fear the Lord, and serve him in sincerity and in truth: and put away the gods which your fathers served on the other side of the flood, and in Egypt; and serve ye the Lord. And if it seem evil unto you to serve the Lord, choose you this day whom ye will serve; wheather the gods which your fathers served that were on the other side of the flood, or the gods of the Amorites, in whose land ye dwell; but as for me and my house, we will serve the Lord.) Now I had to choose: my new job with the most money I had ever made, or a fast with no understanding of why or what I would do after it would be over. Was I sure it was the Lord speaking to me, or was it just my imagination?

That morning, I finally made my decision. I called my boss and told them that I would be resigning, as I would be unable to fulfill my duty any longer. That was it, and I went on to start the fast that morning. I went to get some apple juice to start the fast with, when suddenly I noticed something on its label. It was showing that it was the company's fiftieth year in the apple juice business. Indeed, the Lord confirms his word with the signs. I felt a sense of relief reading that label. Now I knew I was doing his will, and not mine.

For the first week or so of the fast, everything was normal. I was not weak or anything. I even played a round of disc golf, and nobody knew I was fasting. For the Lord said:

> (Matthew 6:16-18; "Moreover when ye fast, Be not, as the hypocrites, of a sad countenance: for they disfigure their faces, that they may appear unto men to fast. Verily I say unto you, They have their reward. But thou, when thou fastest, anoint thine head, and wash thy face; That thou appear not unto men to fast, but unto thy Father which is in secret: and thy Father, which seeth in secret, shall reward thee openly.)

But eventually my strength left me. Despite the physical weakness I was feeling, I would still go visit my mom during the day and do some chores around the house. At this time, I still did not know why I was fasting, but it wouldn't be long enough though before I would. After a few weeks, I started losing weight. My friend, who helped me get in the last job I was in, would stop by and check on me. He had never seen anyone on a fast like this and he could tell that I had lost weight indeed.

One day, my mom called me up with some bad news. She had just gotten back from the doctor, and she was told that her cancer had come back. Six years earlier, she was diagnosed with lung cancer, but with surgery, radiation, chemo treatments and lots of prayer, she had made it through—or so we thought. Now, out of nowhere, it had returned. Her immune system was getting weak, and she had to be careful not to catch a cold or be exposed to anything that would cause infection. I was still about two weeks away from being off the fast, and the doctors wanted her to start chemo immediately. She did one week's worth of the therapy and was terribly sick.

I thought I knew now why the Lord put me on this fast. I thought he wanted me to see that it would be for mom's health, so that she would recover. While I was fasting, mom was also asking the Lord to shorten the fast so I wouldn't be so weak. But weak as I was, I still tried to finish the fast. But I could not make it through the fifty days. I only did forty-eight and a half days of fasting, and I felt like the Lord was cutting it short. Or maybe it was because of my mom's prayers. Nevertheless, it was over, and mom also did not take any more chemo treatments after that week. She was so sick she couldn't take it. She decided to leave it in the Lord's hands.

One Saturday at about midnight, we had a visitation from the Lord. We were already sound asleep, and I was suddenly awakened by music. The music was at a very loud volume. We did not know where it was coming from. It startled me.

I woke Debbie up and we went into the living room, and there we discovered where the music was coming from. We had a stereo with CDs in the CD player, but we had not remembered turning it on nor putting it in full volume. So how did the stereo get turned on? We did not know.

We turned it down, listened for a minute, then turned it off and went back to sleep. But a week later, on exactly the same day and hour the weird incident took place, it happened again. The stereo came on, and we jumped up and went to the living room again. It was the same song that had played the week before. We knew the Lord was showing us something, but we didn't know what it was yet.

Debbie had just finished a book she wanted me to read. It was called *God is Never Late; He's Seldom Early; He's Always Right on Time*, by Stan Toler. I started reading the book and got to a part that, I was sure, the Lord wanted me to see. In 1873 a successful business man named Horatio Spafford lost his earthly goods in the Chicago fire. Spafford weathered that storm reasoning by claiming that his true treasure was in heaven. Just a few weeks later, his wife and four children sailed for France on the *Ville du Havre*. He was to join them a short time later. During the Atlantic crossing, the Ville du Havre was rammed by an English vessel and sank. Two hundred twenty-six souls were lost, including the Spafford children. Spafford was given the news while he was crossing the same ocean and was shown the very spot in the Atlantic where his four children had met their fate. Although stricken with grief, Spafford looked to the Lord for strength. He began to feel a supernatural peace. He recorded that experience in the words of a hymn, now familiar to many who have encountered some troubling times:

> When peace like a river attendeth my way,
> When sorrows like sea billows roll;
> Whatever my lot, thou hast taught me to say,
> It is well, it is well with my soul.

"Though wilt keep him in perfect peace, whose mind is stayed on thee: because he trusteth in thee." (Isaiah 26:3, KJV) When I read this, my heart sank because now I knew what the Lord was telling us. He was getting ready to take mom home, not heal her, but take her. And because the song he had turned on those consecutive weeknights was that very same song, "It Is Well With My Soul." I didn't want to believe it, but I knew it was true. The song was to comfort us during this time, and the Lord was also telling us that it was all right; that we shouldn't be upset that Mom was going to be with him.

A few days leading to mom's departure, many people came to visit her. One of these people had just written a book and had it published. And it was no coincidence that we met, it was the spirit of truth letting me know it was time to write the things I had seen and heard. Mom was at home with her family when she passed away on October 22, 2011. She was buried on the same day of her mom's birthday. And I'm sure Ma Maw was happy to see her. She got the best birthday present ever—her little girl, who had finally come home to her.

FROM THE AUTHOR

God does not always do things the way we think he should or could. But he does things the way he wants and in his own timing. You see, his will for our life is much greater than we could hope or think for ourselves. It's just up to us to hand it over to him. His will, and not ours, be done.

> Mark 14:36; "And he said, Abba, Father, all things are possible unto thee; take away this cup from me: nevertheless not what I will but what thou wilt".

CHILD OF LIGHT

If you are a child of God, a child of the light, you can hardly wait until you hear his voice again. You will always be watching and listening for him. He is the greatest love of all, the light of the world. If you have never felt his love or heard his voice but would like to do so, a simple and honest prayer is what it takes for you to find the greatest relationship you will ever know.

> Lord, I want to hear your voice and know the love that you have for me. I am a sinner, Lord. Forgive me of my sins. I believe that you are the Son of God, and that you died on the cross for me. Jesus, be my Lord and Savior. Thank you, Amen.

My prayer for you today is that the Lord's will be done in your life.

Teach me thy word, oh Lord, for thy word is the truth.